No Lex
12/12

John Elway

by Mark Stewart

ACKNOWLEDGMENTS

The editors wish to thank John Elway for his cooperation in preparing this book. Thanks also to Integrated Sports International for their assistance.

PHOTO CREDITS

All photos courtesy AP/Wide World Photos, Inc. except the following:

Rob Tringali, Jr./Sports Chrome – cover
John Elway – 8, 9, 10 left, 24 bottom left, 36, 37 top, 37 bottom, 46 left
Brigham Young University – 15, 17, 47 top

STAFF

Project Coordinator: John Sammis, Cronopio Publishing
Series Design: The Sloan Group
Design and Electronic Page Makeup: Jaffe Enterprises, and
　　　Digital Communications Services, Inc.

LIBRARY OF CONGRESS CATALOGING-IN-PUBLICATION DATA
Stewart, Mark.
　　John Elway / by Mark Stewart
　　　　p. cm. – (Grolier all-pro biographies)
　　Includes index.
　　Summary: A brief biography of the all-pro quarterback of the Denver Broncos.
　　ISBN 0-516-20145-X (lib. binding)–ISBN 0-516-26009-X (pbk.)
　　1. Elway, John, 1960-　–. Juvenile literature. 2. Football players–United States–Biography–
Juvenile literature. 3. Denver Broncos (Football team)–Juvenile literature. [1. Elway, John, 1960-
2. Football players.] I. Title II. Series
　　GV939.E48S84　1996
　　796.332'092–dc20
　　[B]
96-33788
CIP
AC

Grolier **ALL-PRO** Biographies™

John Elway

by
Mark Stewart

FLINT RIVER REGIONAL LIBRARY

CHILDREN'S PRESS®
A Division of Grolier Publishing
New York • London • Hong Kong • Sydney
Danbury, Connecticut

Contents

Who Am I? 6

Growing Up 8

College Years 14

Road to the Pros 18

The Story Continues 20

Timeline 24

Game Action! 26

Dealing With It 30

How Does He Do It? 32

The Grind 34

Family Matters 36

Say What? 38

Career Highlights **40**

Reaching Out **42**

Numbers **44**

What If **45**

Glossary **46**

Index **48**

Who

Am I?

When you're a kid, saying hello can be just as hard as saying goodbye. I should know. Each time my family moved to a new town, I had to leave my old friends behind and try to make new ones. We moved five times, and it never got any easier. When I decided to become a professional football player, I knew I was entering a world where people get traded from one city to another every day. So what happened? I'm still in the same town where I started! My name is John Elway, and this is my story . . . "

John Elway

"Saying hello can be just as hard as saying goodbye."

Growing Up

John Elway's childhood was probably very different from your own. The Elway family was constantly on the move. John's father, Jack Elway, was a football coach working his way toward a job with a major university. This meant packing up his young family and moving each time he was offered a better position with another team. Every few years, the Elways loaded their belongings on a truck and moved. Altogether, John lived in three states—Washington, California, and Montana—and went to schools in six different towns. He was sad to say goodbye to all of his friends. He found it difficult to make new friends knowing that one day, he would have to say goodbye to them, too.

John (left) with his mother and father

Janet and Jack Elway had three children in all. John has two sisters, and one is his twin. Janna was born just 11 minutes after her brother. Jack Elway taught his son to love all sports, not just football. Much to Jack's delight, John turned out to be a superb athlete. From an early age, John was always one of the best baseball and basketball players in his neighborhood, and he had a powerful, accurate arm. Playing sports created a special bond between John and his father. "I would say that my dad is the most important person to me because of the influence that he's had on me throughout my life. For as long as I can remember, he's been the one I've looked up to, and whenever I've had problems I have always gone to him. Of course, my mom gets a lot of credit, too. She's been great, putting up with two football guys in the house."

Calvin Hill was John's first football hero. John wore number 35 and called himself "Calvin Elway."

John's first football hero was Calvin Hill, the star running back for the Dallas Cowboys. To honor his favorite player, John wore number 35 in a youth football league and called himself "Calvin Elway." Calvin Hill's son, Grant, grew up to be a sports star just like John, but he is not a football player. He is a forward for the Detroit Pistons in the National Basketball Association.

When he reached high school, John switched from playing running back to quarterback because he had such a strong throwing arm. When he switched to quarterback, he found a new football hero, as well. "In high school, my idol was Roger Staubach, who also played for the Cowboys. I liked his style of play. He scrambled a lot and he was really tough. Today, I like to think that I play a little like 'Roger the Dodger.'"

Because his family moved so often, John faced more challenges than most kids encounter in school. John had to transfer to a lot of different schools, and he had to get to know many different classmates and teachers. His favorite teacher was Mr. Anderson in the sixth grade. Mr. Anderson got John excited about projects and helped him whenever he did not understand something. Mr. Anderson also loved sports, just like John. The class kickball game was the highlight of the day.

John was a good student right through junior high school, but when he began taking geometry, he ran into problems. No matter how hard he tried to understand the relationship between numbers and shapes, he got confused. This was especially frustrating because math had always been his favorite subject. With extra help from his teacher, however, John managed to pass.

In other subjects, John did just fine. He enjoyed learning, and he appreciated how important school was. He spent time talking to the older players on his father's college football teams. John realized that many of them did not take education very seriously. John knew that most of them were not

When John became a quarterback, his new hero was Roger Staubach, quarterback of the Dallas Cowboys.

good enough to become pro football players, and he wondered what they would do after football. How in the world would they make a living?

John recalls, "I saw how important it was not just to stay in school, but to work really hard in school. I know that a lot of times kids don't enjoy going to school. But when you look at the big picture, it's only 12 years out of your life, and four more if you decide to go to college. Well, you'll find out that those are the most important years of your life, because what you learn is likely to determine how comfortable the rest of your life will be. Struggling to keep up with your studies is a lot easier than struggling to pay the rent and put food on the table when you don't have a diploma. Reading should be your first priority. The more you read, the better you become at it. And the better a reader you are, the easier it is to communicate with others."

In high school, John continued working hard in the class-room and on the football field. He was determined to become one of the top quarterbacks in the country so he would attract the attention of college football recruiters. Having a football coach for a father helped John a lot. Jack Elway helped his son think like a big-time quarterback. He also made John under-stand that being the best meant making sacrifices. When the other kids were having fun, John would stay behind and prac-tice throwing the football. And after finishing his homework each evening, he put in an extra ho___ game films and memorizing new plays.

John learned early never to g___ t San Fernando High School, he threy___ in the game with 11 seconds left. Th___ od, however, because a penalty was ___ teammates. He went back to the hud___ d teammates and simply told them to ___ n. If they were good enough to pull ___ they were good enough to pull off ___ at they did—Elway threw another lon___ e Grenada Hills High a thrilling victo___

When it ___ n a college, John had a tremendous ___ was from San Jose State___ oached. John surprise___ own his own father___ a scholarship from ___ e school had everything ___ high-powered passing progran ___ one of the best academic programs in the country.

John's father, Jack Elway, was head coach at San Jose State, but John turned down his dad's scholarship offer.

College

John Elway arrived at Stanford University in the fall of 1979 and set about the task of winning the starting quarterback's job. The number he wore in high school, 11, was not available, so he chose number 7 instead. Other than that, things went very smoothly. By the end of his first season, John had become the team's number-one signal caller. By the end of his second season, he was one of the hottest passing prospects in the nation. In his first full season as a starter, he threw for 2,889 yards and 27 touchdowns to lead an average team to a respectable 6 and 5 season.

John's junior and senior seasons were spectacular, too. Despite an ankle injury in 1981, he threw for 2,674 yards and 20 touchdowns. In 1982, he led Stanford to a 43–31 win over the number-one-ranked Washington Huskies and finished second to Herschel Walker of USC in the Heisman Trophy voting. John's 24 touchdown passes were the most by any quarterback

Years

All-American John Elway in action for the Stanford Cardinals.

in the country. His 3,242 passing yards were enough to make him a unanimous All-American.

John completed 62 percent of his passes during his college career—a remarkable figure for a quarterback who threw so hard and so often. He improved steadily from his first season to his last, and broke five college passing records.

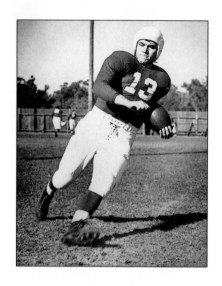  

John was one of four great quarterbacks to play for Stanford. The others were (left to right) Frankie Albert, John Brodie, and Jim Plunkett.

John's father was very proud of his son's accomplishments. But when Stanford played San Jose State, Jack Elway had to forget that his own son was the opposing quarterback. That was not easy in their first two meetings, as John led Stanford to victory both times. The tables turned in 1981, when John had the worst game of his career and was sacked five times by his dad's swarming defense. In their final battle, both father and son had big days. Jack's team won the game, but John had an incredible day, completing 24 of 36 passes for 382 yards and two touchdowns. "I'm glad I'll never have to play against my father again!" groaned John after the 35–31 defeat.

A look at John's college stats and how he improved:

COMPLETIONS

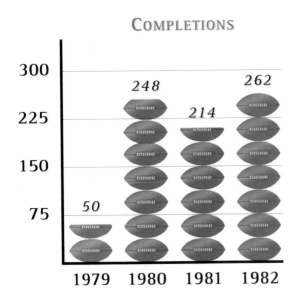

300
225
150
75

1979	1980	1981	1982
50	248	214	262

TOUCHDOWNS

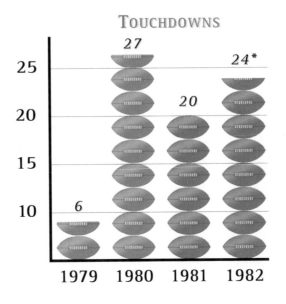

25
20
15
10

1979	1980	1981	1982
6	27	20	24*

*Led nation

John keeps control of a bad snap from center. During his college career, John completed 62% of his passes.

Road to

J ohn Elway was the first pick in the 1983 NFL draft. Most players would be thrilled with the prestige—and money—that goes with being the top selection, but John was unhappy. He had been chosen by the Baltimore Colts, a team that had played so badly the year before that their own fans called them the "Dolts." No matter what the Colts offered, John refused to sign a contract with them.

Baltimore management had no choice but to take John's holdout seriously, for he was a young man with options. The Oakland Invaders of the rival United States Football League had offered him a huge contract, and John had another option: he could play baseball for a

John announces that he will not play for the Baltimore Colts.

the Pros

living. John had been a third baseman and pitcher in high school. He was so good that he had once played minor-league baseball for the New York Yankees one summer and batted .318. John admitted that hitting a home run was a bigger thrill for him than throwing a touchdown, and Yankee scouts were convinced he could be a good major-league power hitter if he gave up football.

Finally, the Colts realized they had no chance of signing John to a contract. They traded him to the Denver Broncos for quarterback Mark Hermann, linebacker Chris Hinton, and Denver's first-round pick in the 1984 draft. The Broncos were a team on the rise. They had a prominent coach, Dan Reeves, promising young talent at almost every position, and a defense led by veterans from Denver's Super Bowl team of 1977. It seemed like the perfect situation for a young quarterback.

Jack Elway (left) joined Dan Reeves's Broncos coaching staff after John joined the team.

19

The Story

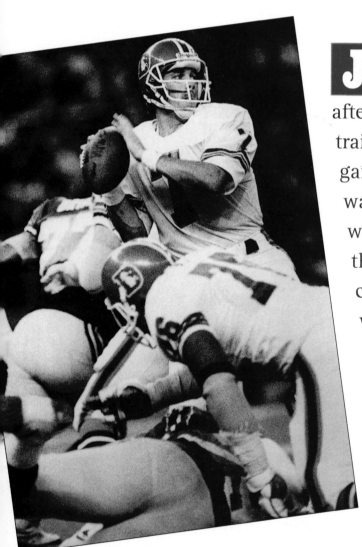

John Elway was named Denver's starting quarterback after an impressive performance in training camp, but within a few games it was clear that the rookie was overmatched. NFL defenders were much bigger and faster than the ones John had faced in college. He sometimes panicked when he looked up and saw defensive alignments he did not recognize. John was benched and told to watch veteran Steve DeBerg very closely. In previous years, DeBerg had

Continues

John reacts to being benched during a poor performance
in his difficult rookie season.

In 1985, John established himself as a top-notch NFL quarterback.

tutored another young quarterback—Joe Montana. By the end of the season, John was back in the lineup and playing well enough to get Denver into the playoffs. That off-season, he literally slept with the team's playbook and watched endless hours of game films. John did not like how it felt to be unprepared in front of 60,000 people, and he vowed it would never happen again.

All the hard work paid off in 1985, when John broke the team records for completions and passing yards. In 1986, the Broncos rode his arm to the division title. Then they stunned the Cleveland Browns in the AFC Championship Game with a dramatic comeback victory to advance to the Super Bowl. There, however they were trounced by the New York Giants, 39–20.

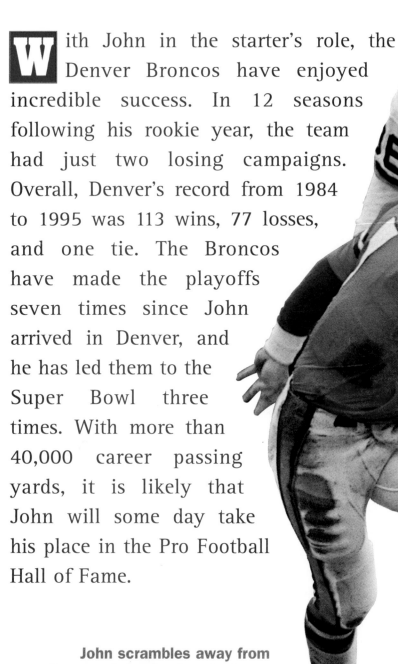

With John in the starter's role, the Denver Broncos have enjoyed incredible success. In 12 seasons following his rookie year, the team had just two losing campaigns. Overall, Denver's record from 1984 to 1995 was 113 wins, 77 losses, and one tie. The Broncos have made the playoffs seven times since John arrived in Denver, and he has led them to the Super Bowl three times. With more than 40,000 career passing yards, it is likely that John will some day take his place in the Pro Football Hall of Fame.

John scrambles away from Browns defender Reggie Camp in the 1986 AFC Championship Game in Cleveland.

Timeline

1979:
Enrolls at
Stanford
University in
Palo Alto,
California

**1983: Drafted by
the Indianapolis
Colts; traded
to the Denver
Broncos**

1978:
Plays his final
year for
Granada Hills
High School in
southern
California

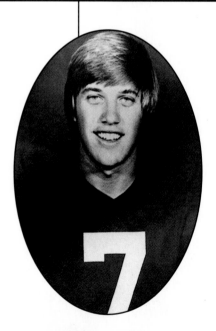

Game

John ranks among the all-time greats when it comes to last-minute comebacks. In the 1986 AFC title game Denver trailed Cleveland 20–13 with 5:43 left on the clock and the ball on their own three-yard line. "We've got 'em just where we want 'em," John joked in the huddle. He marched the team down the field for the tying score, then won the game in overtime. He has pulled out so many games in this fashion that players around the league simply say "We got Elwayed" when it happens to their team!

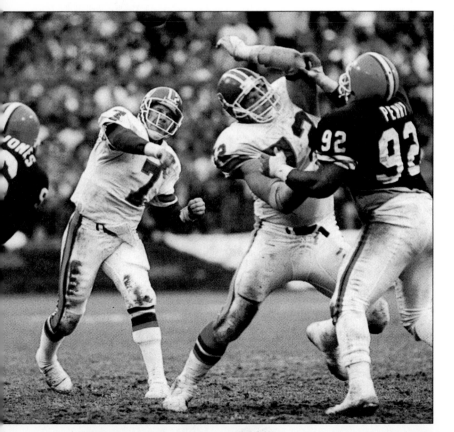

1993:
Records
career high
of 4,030
passing
yards

1987: Leads the
Denver Broncos to
the Super Bowl

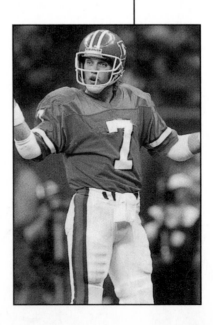

1990:
Returns to the
Super Bowl,
but loses to
San Francisco,
55–10

1984: Leads Broncos
to club-record 13 wins.

Action!

When our backs are against the wall, we always seem to come out of it."

John played a great game in Super Bowl XXII, completing 22 of 37 passes for 304 yards and just one interception. Despite John's performance, the New York Giants beat Denver 39–20.

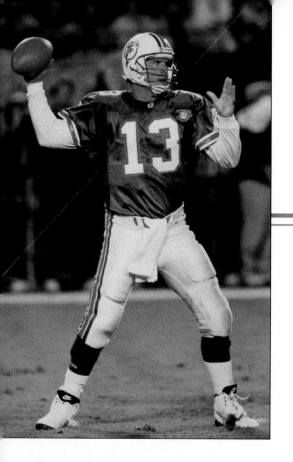

John has topped 3,000 passing yards 10 times in his career. Only Dan Marino (left)—who John thinks is the best passer in football—has reached that plateau more often.

John says, "Practice, dedication, and sacrifice—these are the keys to success. You need to dedicate yourself right from the start to accomplish your goals. It will take time, but it's worth it."

John will not be satisfied until he wins the Super Bowl. "We've won big games. We've had great comebacks . . . but I want to win the Super Bowl ring."

"The thing I'm most proud of is my will to work hard, compete, and win."

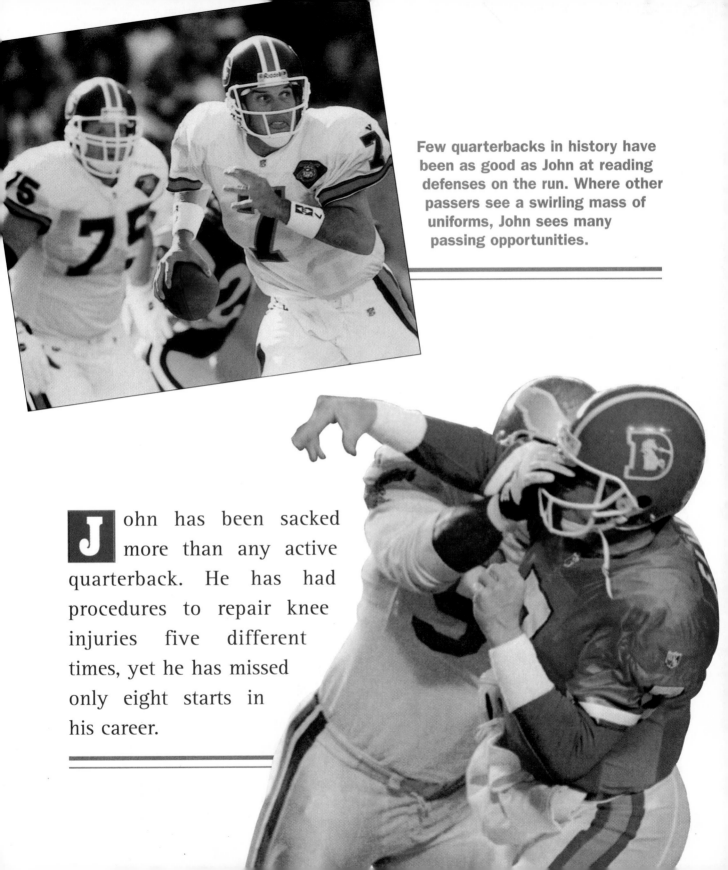

Few quarterbacks in history have been as good as John at reading defenses on the run. Where other passers see a swirling mass of uniforms, John sees many passing opportunities.

John has been sacked more than any active quarterback. He has had procedures to repair knee injuries five different times, yet he has missed only eight starts in his career.

Dealing

Nothing is more embarrassing for a quarterback than throwing an interception. When John Elway threw five against the Kansas City Chiefs in the second-to-last game of the 1985 season, he wanted to dig a hole and crawl inside.

The Broncos needed a win to stay in the playoff race, and John was killing their chances. Rather than give up, he put the interceptions out of his mind, marched back on the field and engineered the drive that gave Denver a 16–13 victory. It was not a pretty win, but the outcome could have been much uglier had John not learned from his mistakes.

With It

Sacks, interceptions, and incomplete passes drive John crazy. Below: John is brought down by Green Bay's Shawn Patterson. Opposite: Raider Chester McGlocton causes an incomplete pass.

HOW DOES

Some of John Elway's biggest fans are actually other NFL quarterbacks. They marvel at how accurate his passes are, no matter how hard or how far he throws them. A bullet pass has to be right on the money or a receiver might not be able to handle it. And a long pass must be timed just right so a

In training, John uses a stopwatch to time his drops and set-ups.

He Do It?

receiver can catch it without breaking his stride. Elway has become a master at both kinds of throws.

"I have always worked on my throwing. In high school, I threw the ball year-round. When other kids were off at the beach in the summer, I would throw 300 balls to my receivers just to be ready for the upcoming season. So I think that just constantly throwing the ball is what has helped me get better and better."

In practice, John uses a stopwatch to make sure he drops back and sets up in the same amount of time. With a perfectly timed drop, John knows where all of his receivers are before he looks up. This way, he does not have to waste time trying to find them. John then picks the open receiver and fires away.

"Your drops have to be precise for the offense to get its timing down. You need to get good depth in the pocket and set up properly each and every time."

The Grind

For many players, the hardest part of pro football is the travel. All of those airplane rides make it very difficult to recover from the bumps, bruises, twists, and sprains that are part of everyday life in the NFL. John Elway finds that it is easier to stay sharp if he keeps a positive attitude about travel.

"I like to think of every trip as an adventure. It's a chance to see new places and meet new people."

London policemen joke with John before a 1987 exhibition game in England against the Rams.

John teaches football technique to Japanese sumo wrestler Masurao.
The Broncos went to Japan in 1990 to play the Seahawks.

Family

In 1994, John married Janet Buchan. They met when they were students at Stanford.

I f there is one athlete in the world who understands the importance of a healthy, happy family, it is John Elway. He and his father, who is now a Broncos scout, see each other almost every day and are still best friends.

Now John has a family of his own. He and his wife, Janet, have four children: Jessica, Jordan, Julianne, and—you guessed it—Jack.

Matters

Sometimes Janet travels with John to games. Here they are on their way to the Pro Bowl in Hawaii.

John, Janet, and their children (left to right) Jack, Julianne, Jessica, and Jordan

Say What?

Here's what football people are saying about John Elway:

"I've chased this guy around the league for the last seven years. I'm just happy that now I will be wearing the same colors as him in the fourth quarter."

—Michael Dean Perry, former Cleveland Brown and current Denver Broncos defenseman

"If number 7 is under center, we always feel like we're going to win."

—Shannon Sharpe, Denver Broncos tight end

"I can think of few athletes that have meant as much to their city as John has to Denver. Maybe Gretzky, maybe Jordan—it's a short list."

—*Pat Bowlen, Denver Broncos owner*

"In the huddle, he has respect right away. He commands it because of who he is."

—*Mike Pritchard, Denver Broncos receiver*

"When you have a quarterback as talented as Elway, you start to think of what you can do to take full advantage of his skills."

—*Wade Phillips, former Denver Broncos head coach*

"He never looks at the sidelines for sympathy. He knows it's part of the game. He just gets up and goes back to the huddle. Believe me, his teammates notice that."

—*Hugh Millen,*
  Denver Broncos backup quarterback

Career

John has reached the AFC Championship Game four times and has only lost once.

In 1995, John came within 30 yards of his second 4,000-yard season. His 3,970 yards were the most by any AFC quarterback.

John is the NFL's "Comeback Kid." He has led the Broncos to victory from fourth-quarter deficits 37 times in his career.

Highlights

John set a Broncos single-game record with 36 completions against the San Diego Chargers in 1994.

John threw touchdown passes in 13 straight games from 1985 to 1986. He nearly repeated the feat with touchdown tosses in 12 straight games from 1992 to 1993.

John salutes the fans after passing the 40,000-yard career mark with a 256-yard performance against the Arizona Cardinals in November 1995. Only five other quarterbacks in history have reached 40,000 yards.

Reaching

People in Denver say that John Elway is as easy to spot around town as the Rocky Mountains. Indeed, he has quarterbacked many good causes for the city over the years. John is a regular speaker at local schools, and he can often be found tossing footballs with kids at charity events in the Mile High City.

"I've also got an organization called the Elway Foundation. We donate money toward the prevention and treatment of child abuse. We started the program back in 1988 and since then, we have given away almost two million dollars."

Wherever John goes, he winds up around kids. Here he meets with children in Tokyo before a game in 1995.

Out

Numbers

Name: John Albert Elway

Nicknames: "Wood" or "Duke"

Born: June 28, 1960

Height: 6' 3"

Weight: 220 pounds

Uniform Number: 7

College: Stanford University

John threw his 200th career touchdown pass in the second game of the 1995 season against the Dallas Cowboys.

Season	Team	Attempts	Completions	Percentage	Yards	Touchdowns
1983	Denver Broncos	259	123	47.5	1,663	7
1984	Denver Broncos	380	214	56.3	2,598	18
1985	Denver Broncos	605*	327	54.0	3,891	22
1986	Denver Broncos	504	280	55.6	3,485	19
1987	Denver Broncos	410	224	54.6	3,198	19
1988	Denver Broncos	496	274	55.2	3,309	17
1989	Denver Broncos	416	223	53.6	3,051	18
1990	Denver Broncos	502	294	58.6	3,526	15
1991	Denver Broncos	451	242	53.7	3,253	13
1992	Denver Broncos	316	174	55.1	2,242	10
1993	Denver Broncos	551*	348*	63.2	4,030*	25
1994	Denver Broncos	494	307	62.1	3,490	16
1995	Denver Broncos	542	316	58.3	3,970	26
Total		5,926	3,346	56.5	41,706	225

* Led League

What If...

I hurt my knee when I was in high school and had to undergo surgery in my senior year. I rehabilitated it as best I could and tried to remain positive, but sometimes I wondered what life would be like if I was unable to play football again. Luckily, I made a full recovery and was able to get a college scholarship. But the experience made me take my education extra seriously. I enjoyed math and working with numbers, so I went for a degree in economics. I suppose if football hadn't worked out, I would be an accountant today."

Glossary

DEFICIT disadvantage; loss

DEJECTED feeling a loss of spirit; saddened

ECONOMICS the study of how a person, company, or nation uses money

FLOURISH to thrive; to grow better and better

ACADEMIC concerning education and learning

ACCOUNTANT a person who takes care of the finances and taxes of an individual or company

ACCURATE exact; correct

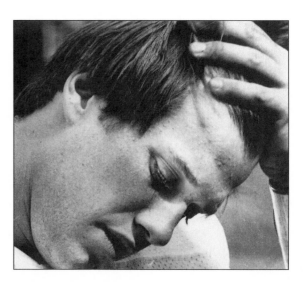

INFLUENCE to sway; to make an impression on someone

MARVEL to become full of surprise, wonder, and astonishment

MEDIOCRE so-so; ordinary

MILE HIGH CITY Denver's nickname; Colorado's capital is located in the Rocky Mountains and is approximately one mile above sea level

PLATEAU a level of high accomplishment

PRECISE exact; correct

PRESTIGE respect

PRIORITY first in importance

PROSPECT one who shows the ability to grow into a certain role; a candidate

RECRUITER one who tries to get people to join their team or organization

SCHOLARSHIP money given to a student to help pay for schooling

ULTIMATE the greatest; the best

UNANIMOUS everyone in agreement

VETERAN one who has had a lot of experience

Index

AFC Championship Game, 22, 26, 40
Albert, Frankie, 16
Baltimore Colts, 18–19
Bowlen, Pat, 39
Brodie, John, 16
California, 8
Cleveland Browns, 22, 26
Dallas Cowboys, 10, 44
DeBerg, Steve, 20–22
Denver Broncos, 19–23, 26, 30, 38–39, 41, 44
Denver, Colorado, 42
Detroit Pistons, 10
Elway Foundation, 42
Elway, John
 and awards/honors won, 14–15
 childhood of, 7–13
 education of, 10–13, 45
 family of, 7, 8–9, 36–37
 injuries of, 14
 statistics of, 17, 44
 uniform number of, 10, 14
Grenada Hills High School, 13
Heisman Trophy, 14
Hermann, Mark, 19
Hill, Calvin, 10
Hill, Grant, 10
Hinton, Chris, 19
Kansas City Chiefs, 30

Marino, Dan, 28
Millen, Hugh, 39
Montana, 8
Montana, Joe, 22
National Basketball Association (NBA), 10
National Football League (NFL), 18
New York Giants, 22, 27
New York Yankees, 19
Oakland Invaders, 18
Perry, Michael Dean, 38
Phillips, Wade, 39
Plunkett, Jim, 16
Pritchard, Mike, 39
Pro Football Hall of Fame, 23
Reeves, Dan, 19
San Diego Chargers, 41
San Fernando High School, 13
San Jose State University, 13, 16
Sharpe, Shannon, 38
Stanford University, 13, 14–17, 44
Staubach, Roger, 10, 11
Super Bowl, 19, 22, 23, 27, 28
United States Football League, 18
Walker, Herschel, 14
Washington, 8

About The Author

Mark Stewart grew up in New York City in the 1960s and 1970s—when the Mets, Jets, and Knicks all had championship teams. As a child, Mark read everything about sports he could lay his hands on. Today, he is one of the busiest sportswriters around. Since 1990, he has written close to 500 sports stories for kids, including profiles on more than 200 athletes, past and present. A graduate of Duke University, Mark served as senior editor of *Racquet*, a national tennis magazine, and was managing editor of *Super News*, a sporting goods industry newspaper. He is the author of every Grolier All-Pro Biography.